Now you see it...

STRING GAMES AND STORIES
BOOK 2

Michael Taylor

Published by Hawthorn Press, Copyright © 2002
Hawthorn House, 1 Lansdown Lane, Stroud, Gloucestershire,
GL5 1BJ. UK
Tel. (01453) 757040 Fax. (01453) 751138
E-mail: info@hawthornpress.com
Website: **www.hawthornpress.com**

Typeset at Hawthorn Press by Lynda Smith
Cover design by Patrick Roe at Southgate Solutions
Back cover photograph reproduced by kind permission of Keith Walter, Surrey and Sussex Newspapers
Printed by The Cromwell Press, Trowbridge, Wiltshire

A catalogue record of this book is available from the British Library Cataloguing in Publication Data

ISBN 1 903458 21 8

CONTENTS

CONTENTS

FOREWORD

According to astrophysicist John Gribbin 'everything in the universe is made of string.' The string metaphor is commonly used by quantum physicists to describe the cosmos! And you can gain personal experience of this by enjoying Michael Taylor's string games and stories.

Michael's approach highlights 'everyday magic', one of the most potent aspects of creating string games – you can look at the commonplace with new eyes. Even when you show a string trick step by step, it still creates magic!

I have been storytelling in string since 1980, fascinated by what can be formed and suggested by a simple loop of cord. Having established a 'vocabulary' of more than 150 different figures from around the world, I present and share them in a show called 'Stringeries'. People are often awed by the complexity and sheer beauty of string figures that sometimes originate far away and may be hundreds of years old.

Michael has added a kind of 'down home' exoticism to string art, making the specialness and strangeness of string art accessible to everyone.

I also fold paper using the Japanese practice of origami. Sometimes while folding I stop before finishing a model to examine a shape to ask myself or the audience what it suggested. Michael, through his own creations, has made this type of reflection into a veritable art form. With each manipulation he challenges our imagination to 'see' the kaleidoscope of reality with the innocence of a child – a circle of string becomes the sun or a soap bubble; another loop of string opens into a book before becoming a little girl and then a necklace. And the whole is neatly inserted into a story that permits the whole to flow. This flows from finger to finger and from artist to spectator who in turn will take up a string to become the performer.

There are many expressions that connect language expressions to string and thread – one can be tied up in knots or know the ropes, spin a yarn or weave a lie. In Michael Taylor's strings and stories, you are invited to take a speaking part in this special link that makes us human.

So the next time you find a piece of string on the ground, don't throw it away. But rather draw it close to your ear and listen, for I'm sure it will have its story to tell!

Sam Cannarozzi
Storyteller and String Artist

INTRODUCTION
THE STORY OF STRING GAMES

String games are designs woven between the hands with a loop of string. Often songs and stories are associated with the string figures which can be quite complex. They can depict moving animals, people, plants, stars or mythical events.

The figures are very ancient, existing in the Americas, Oceania and Africa possibly since Stone Age times and Europe at least since the tea and spice trades in the seventeenth century when cat's cradle was brought to Europe from South East Asia.

At the end of the nineteenth century anthropologists started to learn, record and share string games. They discovered too the wonderful way string games could 'break the ice', cross language barriers and forge trust and friendship.

During the age of sea travel in the first half of the twentieth century 'string bands' were formed to while away the long hours on board ship with learning and sharing string figures.

Travellers are still fond of playing string games, especially during long train journeys and in airport lounges.

Today when playground crazes occur the figures come from any and every tradition and the children's inventions depict such things as trampolines, computers and space shuttles.

Why do string games survive? The reasons are many: They link the generations. They provide exercise for the imagination, the memory and finger dexterity. They improve children's self-esteem and sociability. They feed our love for magic and story-telling. They give our hands and fingers something clever and artistic to do!

My own String Story

I was first introduced to string games by my father who showed me the Palm Trick (given in this book) and then by my primary school teacher who showed me the Slippery Eel (see Book Three).

It was not until I was a teacher and doing a gymnastics and movement course that I encountered string games again, and was reminded how magical they could be for children – especially when I introduced them to my class the next day.

They showed so much interest that I decided to learn more. I also discovered that these games exist in most cultures and that they can be very complex.

I found that linking the figures together in stories made them easier to remember and more entertaining. Then in response to demands for books on the subject I started writing *Pull the other one!*

After writing Book One I joined the International String Figures Association, discovering that there are many other people around the world who are interested in the subject, and that alongside the traditional figures still being collected, new figures are also being invented all the time.

A Note about the Drawings

Strings have sometimes been drawn shorter and thicker than they really are and hands more face-on than they would normally be in order to show relative positions more clearly.

Drawing strings going under and over each other is very much like drawing Celtic Knots... an ancient art in itself. Traditional artists have long found the process and results quite satisfying and readers might want to try it out on their own figures. Of course, if you want to also draw the hands... especially the writing hand... that is another problem!

How To Use This Book

1. As a Story Book
This book can be read as an illustrated story book – just read the large-typed pages and use a little imagination with the illustrations.

2. As a Colouring Book
See if you can follow the direction of the string around the loop and get back to where you started from. When you have worked it out you can colour the strings to show the form more clearly.

3. As an Instructional Manual for Learning String Games
Just pull out the string and follow the instructions. If you want you can make the same figure with a friend, one player using the right hand while the other uses the left.

3. For Telling Stories while Making String Games
Although it is great fun just making the figures it is more entertaining if you say a few words at the same time. On the Island of Lifu, New Caledonia, they say, 'Come along, Porker' and 'Porker, him go' as they move the pig back and forth; and 'Down she goes' where in this book the boy pulls his jumper over his head.

4. As a Springboard for the Imagination
As soon as you know a few string games you can try out some variations and invent your own stories and figures. If you make up some good ones send them to me,

Michael Taylor, 9 Kidbrooke Rise, Forest Row, East Sussex, RH18 5LA, UK. If your figure or story is chosen for inclusion in a future book you'll get your name in print... and a free copy in the post!

An Introduction to
String Games

THE MONKEY CHAIN

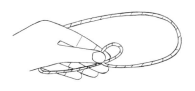

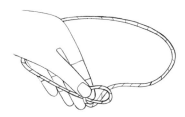

1. Make a small loop in the string. (A 'magnifying glass').

2. Place this small loop over the uppermost continuation of string close to the loop. ('Examine the string').

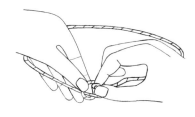

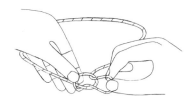

3. Pull this string through the small loop a short way...

...making a new small loop.

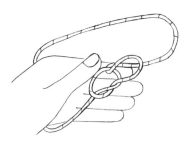

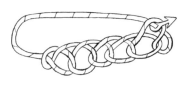

4. Place this new loop over the string again.

5. Repeat the process until you have made the 'Monkey Chain'.

A simple loop of string...

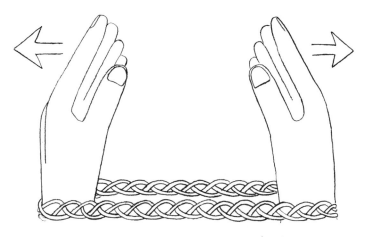

Now you see it...Now you don't.
Pull apart to make the chain unravel...
or wear it as a head band!

A JUMPING FISH

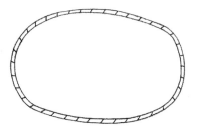

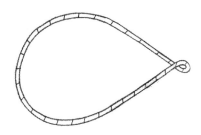

1. Make a 'puddle' on the ground. (Big enough to stand in!)

2. Twist one side to make a 'water drop'.

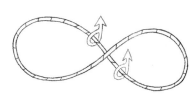

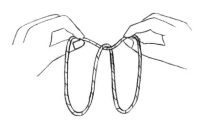

3. Enlarge the 'water drop' to make a figure of eight.

4. Lift the 'water' on either side of the 'bridge'.

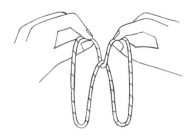

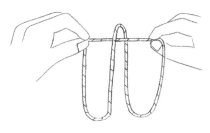

5. Bring the hands together...

and apart to make the 'jumping fish'.

...can turn into anything.

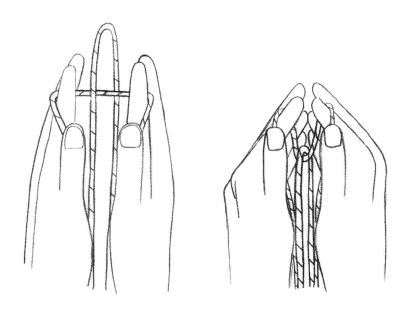

THE SPITTING DRAGON
Make the Jumping Fish. Pinch the short horizontal string
between index and middle fingers and open and close hands to
make the Dragon spit!

A WALKING CARIBOU

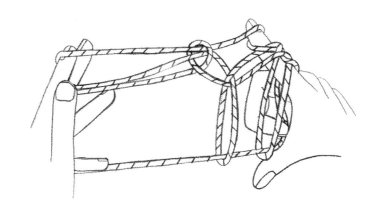

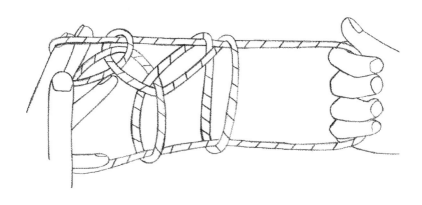

THE CARIBOU
An Inuit string figure from Baffin Island.
It walks from one hand to the other.

Many of the figures move.

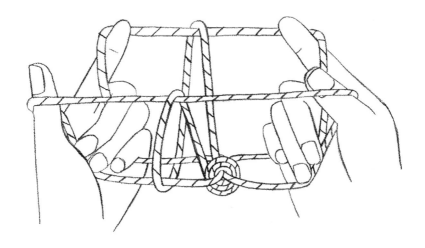

THE NAVAHO BUTTERFLY
It can slowly open and close its wings.

THE MAGIC HANDSHAKE

A great way to give out strings!

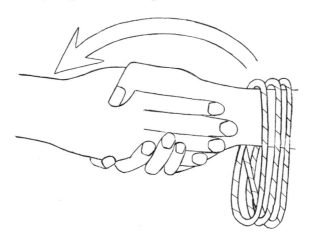

Wind the string a few times round your wrist, shake hands and say, 'Pleased to meet you!'

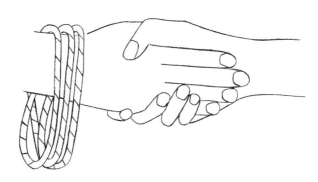

Shake the string onto your friend's wrist, look surprised and say, 'Oh...you have a string already!'

Now it is your turn to make some string figures.

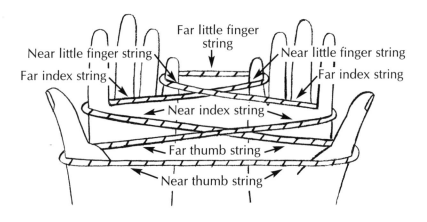

NAMES OF STRINGS

THE BOW AND ARROW

BENDING THE BOW

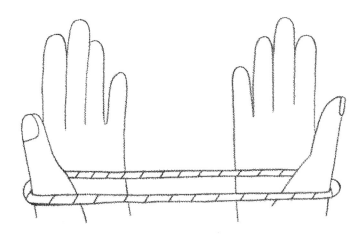

THE BRANCH

Hold the string looped between the thumbs. This represents a stick. Clench the fists and bring hands slightly together to show the stick bending. Make it look as if you are making a huge effort to achieve this!

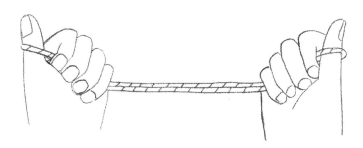

GETTING HOLD OF THE BRANCH

Once a man took a branch.

He tested it, saying,

'That will do fine!'

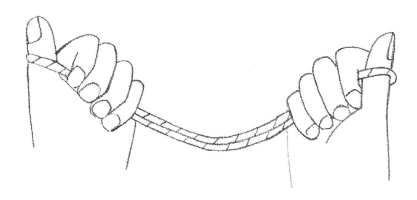

BENDING THE BOW

FIXING SOME TWINE

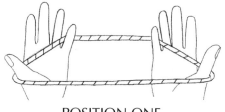

Open fists. Little fingers enter and widen thumb loops from below for Position One.

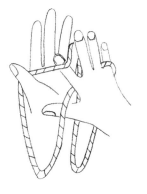

Right index enters left palm string from below and rotates in a clockwise circle, twisting the string in the process.

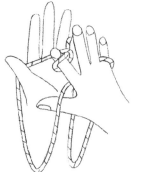

Pull the string out slightly.

28

Then he fixed some twine.

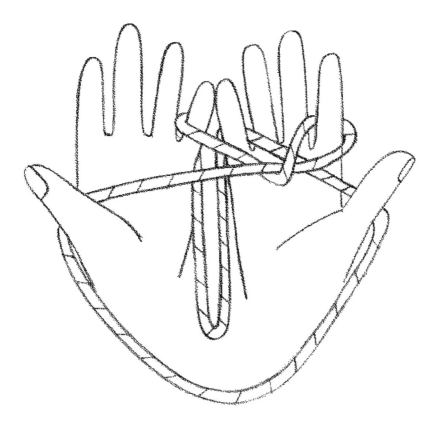

FIXING SOME TWINE

SHOOTING THE ARROW

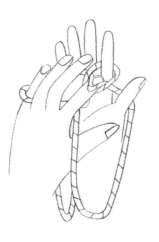

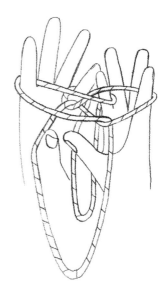

Left index picks up right palm
string from below, between the
index strings and draws out
slightly.

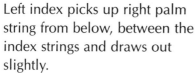

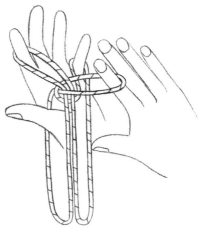

Release right thumb and little finger loops and extend to show
the flying arrow (opposite page).

And shot an arrow.

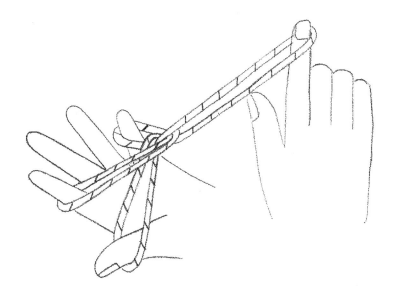

ARROW

THE TREE

Hold arrow point downwards to show the 'Tree'. Release left thumb and left little finger to show something falling from the tree.

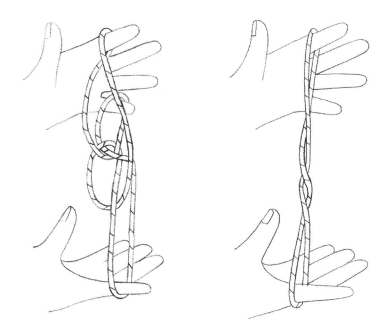

SOMETHING FALLING

...into a tree.

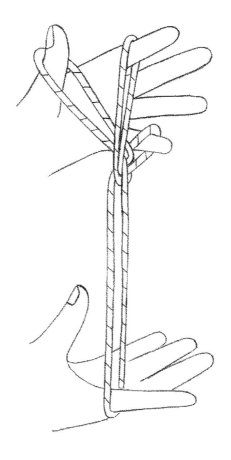

THE TREE

MAN CLIMBING A TREE

OPENING 'A'

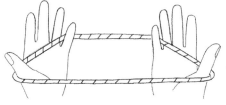

POSITION ONE

Thumbs hold loop. Little fingers enter and widen thumb loops from below for Position One.

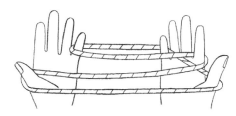

Right index enters left palm string from below and draws out.

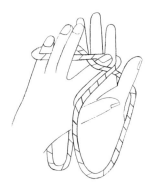

Left index enters right palm string from below and between index strings.

Draw out to make Opening 'A'.

Once a man decided to climb a tall tree.

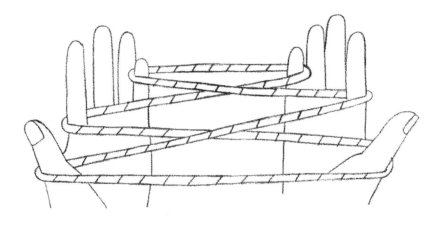

OPENING 'A'

CAUGHT ON BRAMBLES

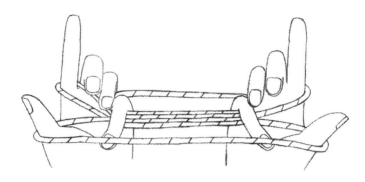

DUCKING HIS HEAD
Little fingers pick up near thumb strings from underneath (after going over index and far thumb strings).

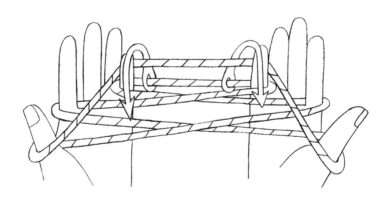

CAUGHT ON BRAMBLES
Opposite hands take turns lifting the lower little finger loops over the upper little finger loops and off the finger.
Make sure that you take the lower loops from the far side so they get caught on the palm strings when dropped on the inside of the hands.

He ducked his head

under the lowest branch

and got caught on some

brambles. He lifted

these off.

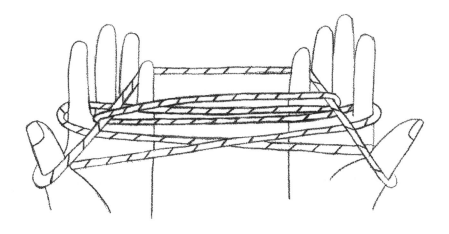

FREED FROM BRAMBLES

PUTTING HIS FOOT DOWN

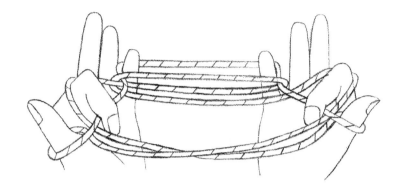

Hook index fingers over palm string (keep two long strings on the near side and four on the far side).

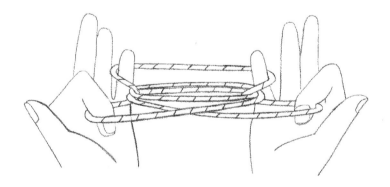

Keep hooked string and little finger string but lose index and thumb strings. Place a foot on the far little finger string.

Then he put his foot at the foot of the tree and started to climb.

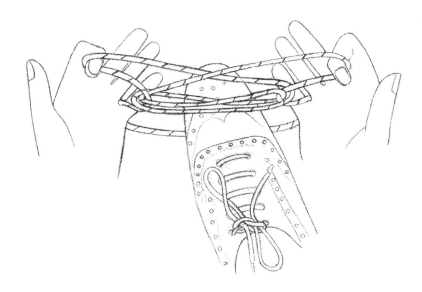

PUTTING HIS FOOT DOWN

CLIMBING UP

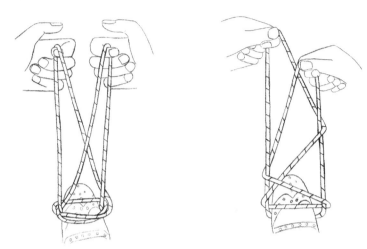

Release little fingers. Pinch side strings with thumbs and index fingers. Release a few centimetres on one side, then the other, with each line of the verse. Repeat as necessary until the man reaches the top. Remember to stop and shiver on the way up.

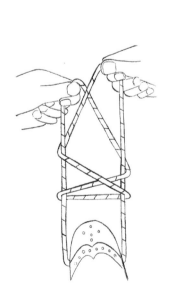

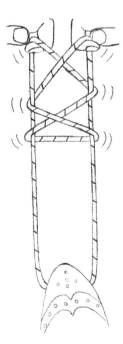

Up...he climbed

One step...at a time

One hand

...then the other

The bark...fell

And the leaves...shivered

He stopped.

He shivered!

Up...he climbed...

All the way to the top!

THE LITTLE PIG

THE GATE

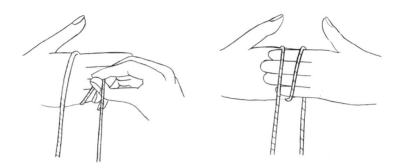

DOUBLE THE STRING by winding a single strand twice around your palm and lifting it.

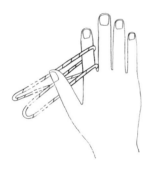

Place the doubled loop on right index on either side of the middle knuckle.

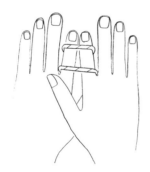

Put left index into doubled loop alongside right index.

Pull hands apart to form the MURRAY OPENING (Gate). Make sure that the parallel strings are on the near side and the cross is on the far side.

This is the gate

to the farm.

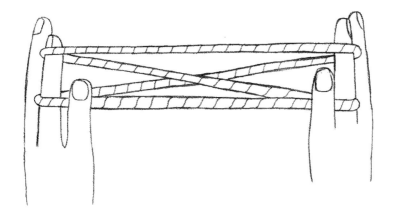

THE GATE

THE GATE TO THE BARN

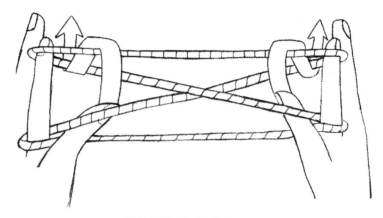

CLIMBING THE GATE

Thumbs (boys) go over the lower parallel string and under the lower crossed strings which they lift up.

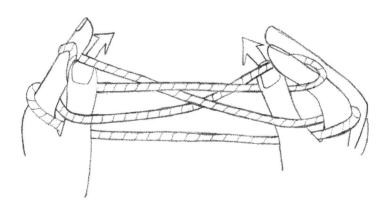

Thumbs repeat the movement over the upper parallel string and under the upper crossed strings which they lift up. Stretch thumbs away from index fingers to show the BARN.

Two boys climb the gate

and go into the barn.

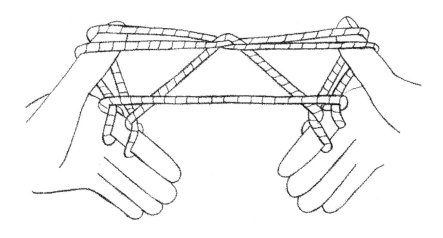

THE BARN

THE BARN TO THE PIG HOUSE

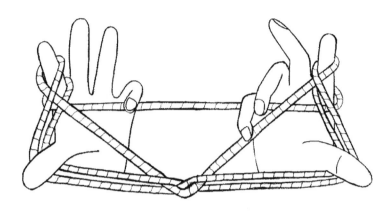

Turn palms to face you and bend little fingers over the diagonal strings.

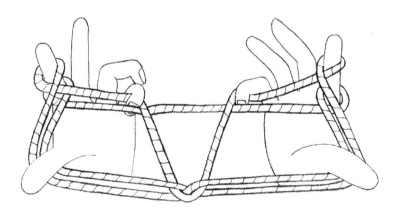

Hook these strings back and tuck the little fingers under the straight single string.

Return to Basic Position (hands ready to clap) to show the PIG HOUSE.

They pass the

pig house.

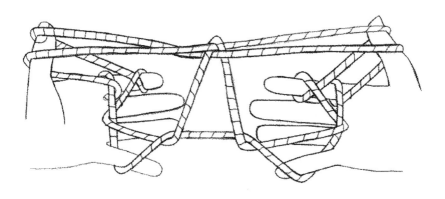

PIG HOUSE

PIG HOUSE TO WATER TROUGH

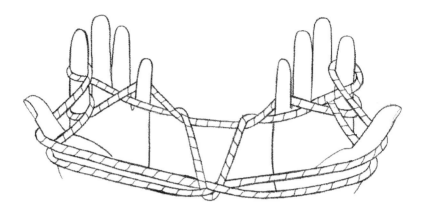

Index fingers dive down into the triangle near the little fingers and lift up the central string (the little finger palm string). When index fingers are fully extended release thumb strings to make the WATER TROUGH.

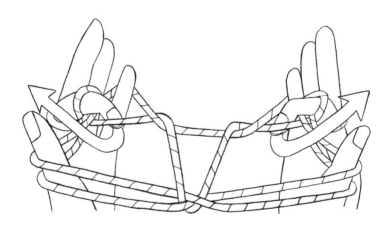

and the water trough.

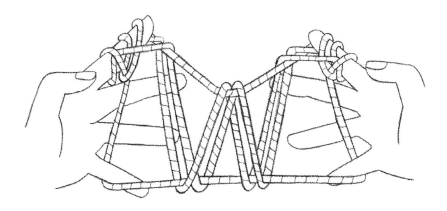

WATER TROUGH

WATER TROUGH TO EGGS

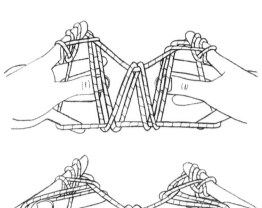

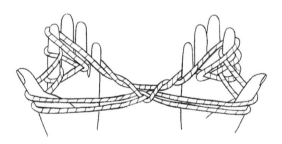

Thumbs lift the sides of the 'W' on their backs.

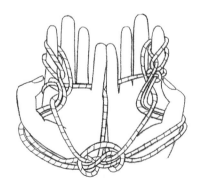

Cup hands together and push off index loops to show EGGS.

They collect

six eggs.

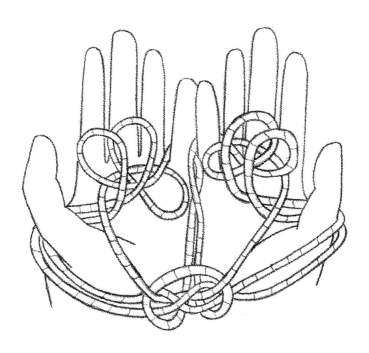

SIX EGGS

EGGS TO CHICKEN HOUSE
TO CAT'S WHISKERS

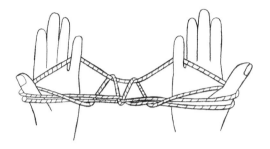

Eggs disappear and
CHICKEN HOUSE
appears as hands pull
apart.

CHICKEN HOUSE

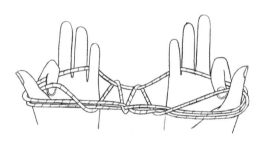

Index fingers pick up
far thumb string from
below and from the
far side.

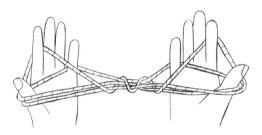

Release thumbs for
CAT'S WHISKERS.

...from the chicken house

and they meet a cat with

long whiskers.

MIAOW!

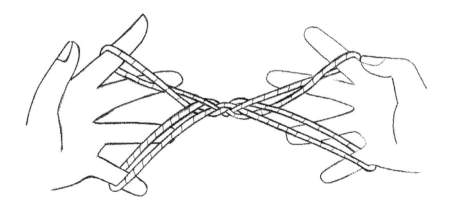

CAT'S WHISKERS

CAT'S WHISKERS TO BOY

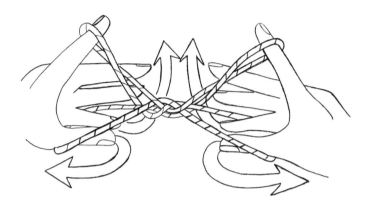

Thumbs go under index loops and enter little finger loops from beneath. Thumbs push far strings down and away, catching them on their backs as they return.

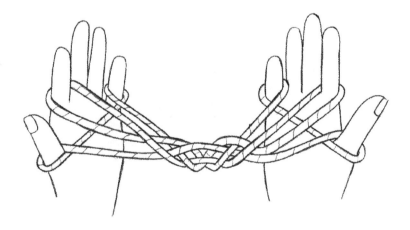

Hold left hand vertically and above right hand to show BOY. Left thumb can tap left little finger to show him clapping! Note the colour of his sleeves and neck.

The first boy stands up

and looks around.

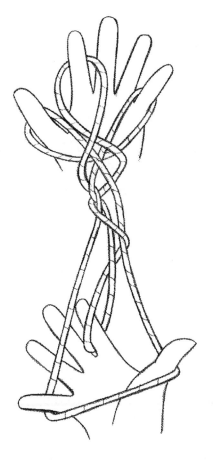

THE BOY

CHANGING A JUMPER

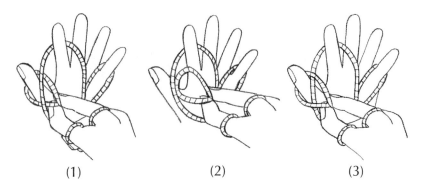

(1) (2) (3)

Right index and thumb enter left index loop (1), lift off the left thumb loop (2), pull this through the index loop and replace it on the thumb (3).

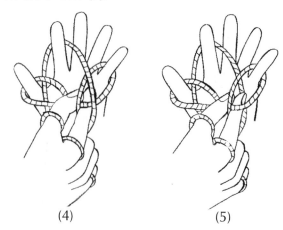

(4) (5)

Likewise the right index and thumb take the left little finger loop (4) through the left index and replace it on the left little finger (5).

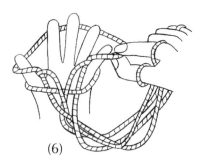

(6)

The left index loop is taken off and placed over the whole left hand (6). The right hand is placed uppermost to show the second boy.

Note the different colours of sleeves and neck.

He changes his jumper

saying: 'One arm,

two arms, over the head!'

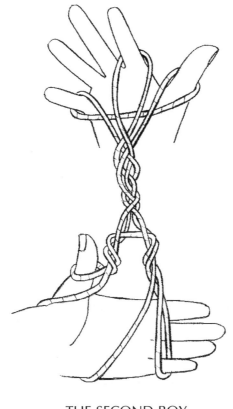

THE SECOND BOY

THE OTHER BOY CHANGES HIS JUMPER

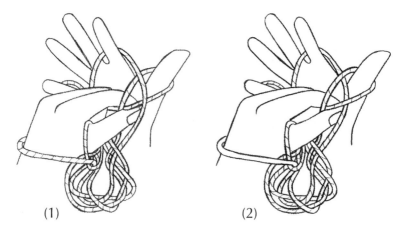

(1)   (2)

Left index and thumb take off right thumb loop (1), bring it through the right index loop and replace it on the thumb (2).

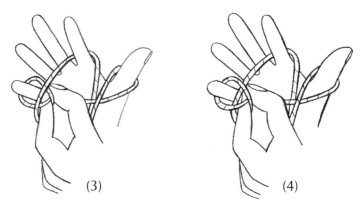

(3)   (4)

Left index and thumb take off right little finger loop (3), bring it through the right index loop and replace it on the little finger (4). The right index loop is placed over the right hand (opposite page).

PLAY SPOT THE DIFFERENCE
You might wish to play 'Spot the Difference' with the pictures on this page!

The second boy

changes a jumper too,

saying: 'One arm,

two arms, over the head!'

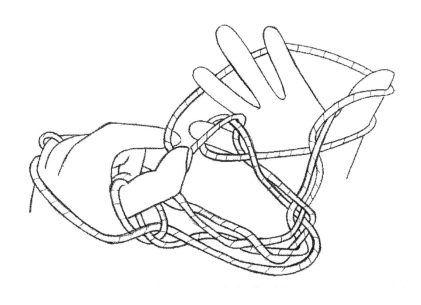

OVER THE HEAD

THE FOOD TROUGH AND BAG

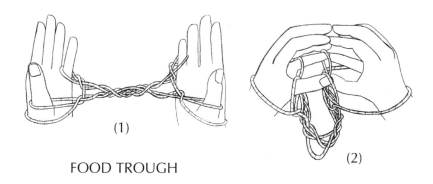

(1)

FOOD TROUGH

(2)

Hands held in the Basic Position hold the FOOD TROUGH (1). Tips first, right thumb and little finger give their loops to the left thumb and little finger (2 and 3).

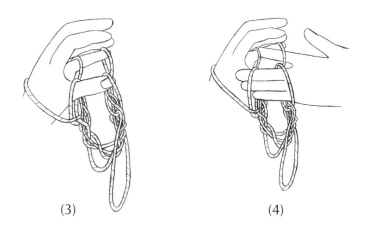

(3)

(4)

Remove right hand.
Tips first, right little, ring and middle fingers take left thumb loops, and right index takes left little finger loops (4) so that the left hand can be removed.
Remember to shake the food bag!

They check that the food

trough is full and

they shake the food bag.

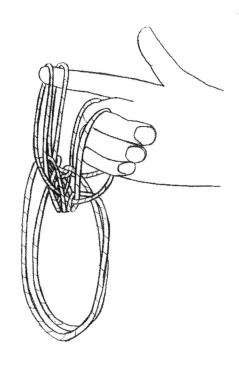

SHAKING THE FOOD BAG

THE PIG APPEARS

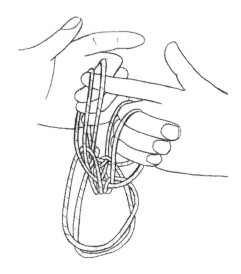

Left fingers take right index loops from knuckle-side.

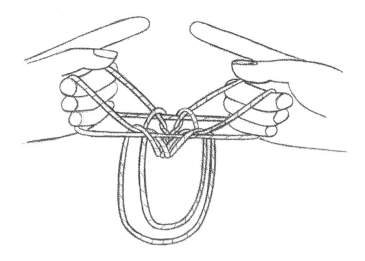

Strings held in fists pull apart firmly and several times to make
THE PIG.

Suddenly a pig jumps

up out of the mud.

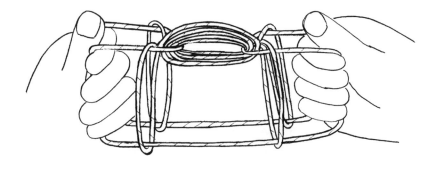

THE PIG

AND DISAPPEARS

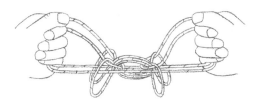

To make the pig splash its tummy in the mud turn the top of your fists slightly together.

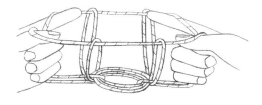

To turn the pig upside down pull legs outwards and up.

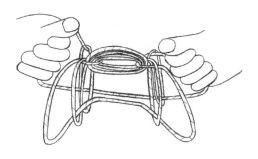

To make the pig disappear drop near strings and pull.

Now repeat the sequence to find the pig, saying: 'It's not by the gate, not in the barn, not in the pig-house, nor in the water trough. It hasn't broken any eggs. It's not in the chicken house. The cat says: Miaow. The boys change their jumpers again. It's not in the food trough. Shake the bag...Here it is! It was in the mud all the time!'

It dances about,

splashing them with

mud.

Then it lies down with

its feet in the air!

Then it gets up again

and disappears.

Where is the pig?

THE LITTLE BAT

IVY

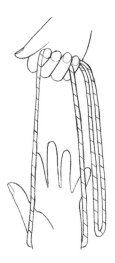

Place the left hand, palm uppermost, in the hanging loop held up by the right hand.

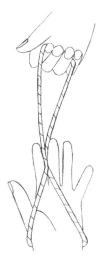

Pass both strings down between the left index and middle fingers and back up, untwisted, on either side of the left index and middle fingers (opposite page).

In the forest

ivy squeezes between

and around the

tree trunks.

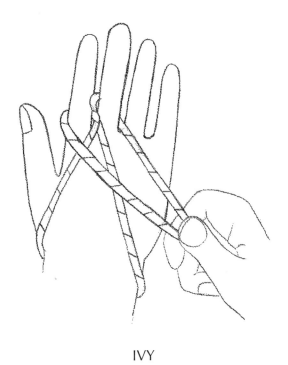

IVY

TWISTING VINES

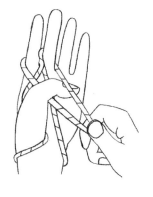

Left thumb picks up far middle finger string from below.

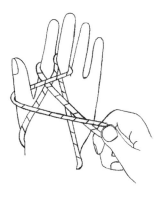

Left little finger picks up near index string from below.

It twists this

way and that.

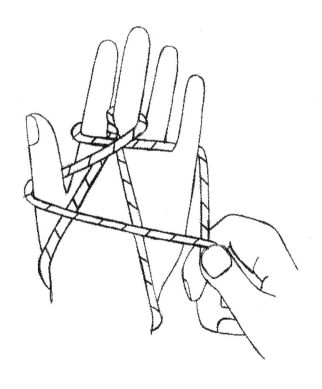

TWISTING VINES

SWINGING VINES, ROOTS AND FRUIT

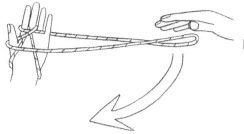

Drop right hand strings.

SWINGING VINE

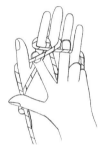

Right middle and index fingers pull out near little and far thumb strings.

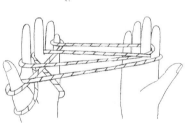

PULLING OUT ROOTS

Right hand lifts off left back-of-hand string over all four fingers and thumb, and drops it.

Vines swing and two men
walk through the forest.
They pull out roots, lift off
brambles and gaze up at
fruit.

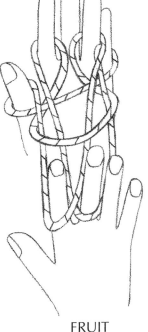

FRUIT

THE BIG BAT

ROOF OF THE CAVE

Finger tips touch with arms raised above the head to indicate the roof of the cave.

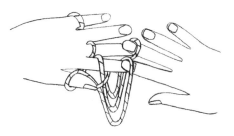

Tip to tip, place right middle and index loops on left middle and index fingers.

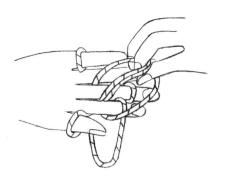

Lift lower middle and index loops over upper loops and off the hand.

They go into a dark cave
and see something moving.
It is a big bat with folded
wings.

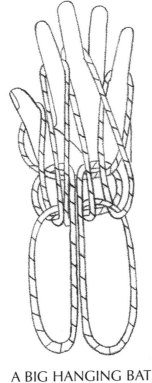

A BIG HANGING BAT

THE LITTLE BAT

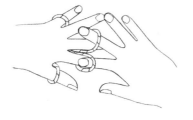

Pass the left index and middle loops to the right index and middle fingers and raise the right hand to make the LITTLE BAT.

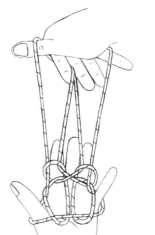

To improve the shape and prepare for flight, squeeze right index and middle together and widen their loops with the thumb and little finger respectively.

THE LITTLE BAT

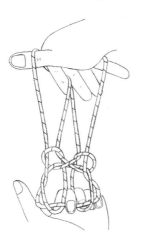

To free the bat's wings gently hook down with the left index the left palm string located between the wings. Release left thumb and little finger, pull palm string through the wings and replace the left thumb and little finger in the loop.

And a small bat, twitching,

ready to open its wings,

flap and fly away.

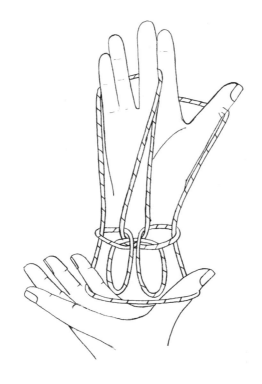

READY TO FLY

FLYING AWAY

Thumbs stretch away from little fingers to open wings.
Both hands shake slowly to flap wings.
Right hand moves away from left to make bat fly away.
As bat reaches right hand, tuck the right thumb in behind the
bat and release other right fingers.
Look into the right distance as if the bat has flown away.

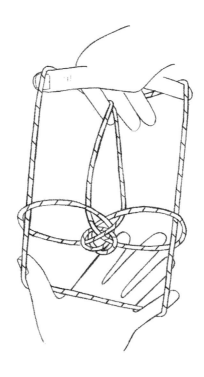

OPENING ITS WINGS

There it goes!

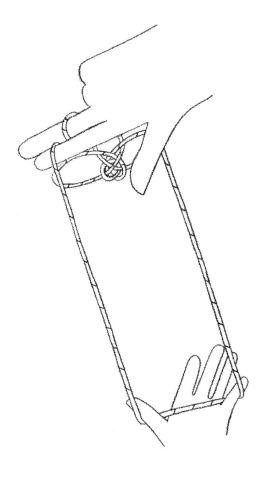

FLYING AWAY

THE RACING CAR

A WORM FOR THE BABY BIRD

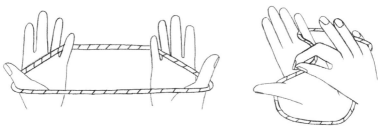

POSITION ONE
Make Position One and release right thumb.
The Bird's Beak (right thumb and index) enters the left palm
string from above.

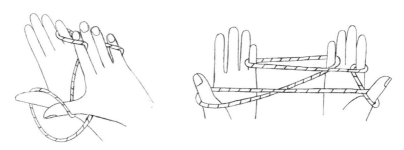

It opens widely, and returns.

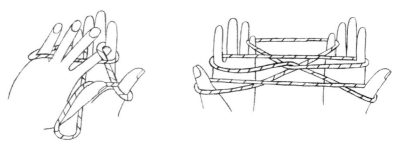

Worm (left index) enters right index loop from below on the far
side of the long index string.
Hands pull apart.

Here is a bird's beak

digging for worms.

Here is a worm

for a baby bird.

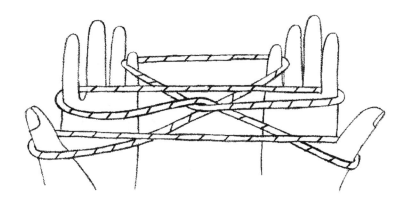

A BIG HANGING LEAF

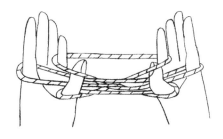

Thumbs go over index strings to pick up near little finger strings from below and return.

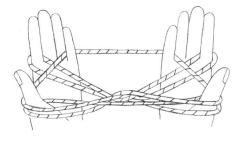

Middle fingers go over index strings to pick up far thumb string from below and return, squeezing the string between middle and index finger tips.

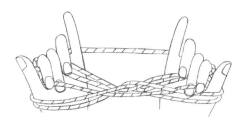

Drop thumb and little finger loops to show a big hanging leaf.

Do not pull apart.

Other birds fly

away and back

among the big leaves.

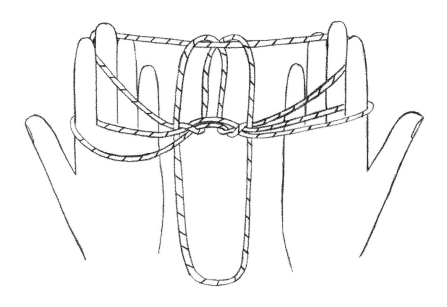

A BIG HANGING LEAF

THE BIRD'S NEST

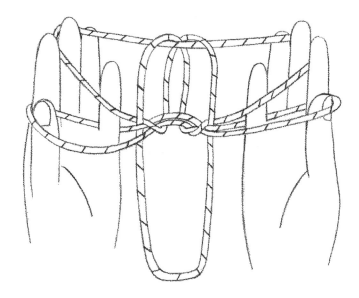

Thumbs and little fingers enter index loops from beneath to make the BIRD'S NEST.

Make sure that strings between middle and index fingers remain firmly held.

If preferred, hook little finger string down with closed ring and little fingers instead of as shown.

SPOT THE DIFFERENCES
Compare the picture on this page with the picture on the previous page!

Behind one big leaf

is a nest.

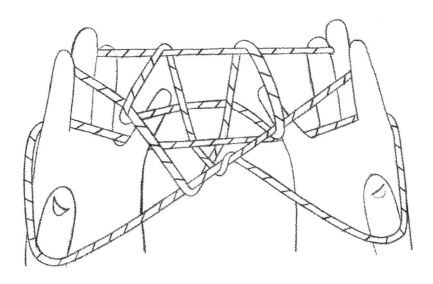

THE BIRD'S NEST

THE RACING CAR

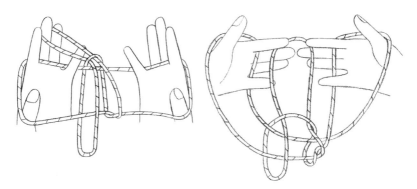

Keep string held between left index and middle taut.
Turn nest opening away and drop the string held between the right index and middle. Part of the nest falls to form an over-sized front wheel. Right index takes the dropped string again by entering left middle finger loop from below on the far side and pulls this string taut.

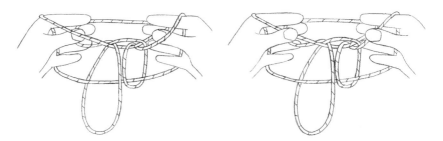

As back wheel shape forms right thumb removes itself from its loop and presses two central strings against the middle finger releasing the right index in the process. Shrink over-sized front wheel and lift back of car by lifting up far string with right index. Allow movement of string especially between left index and middle. Left thumb can replace left index, pinching middle finger string to hold front of car.

92

The nest was built

near a racing track.

Here is a racing car.

READY …STEADY…

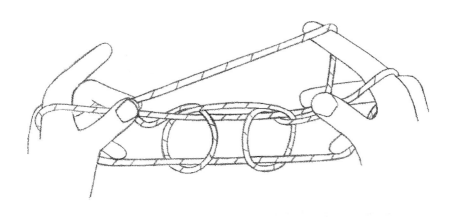

THE RACING CAR

THE DRIVER

To make the car disappear let go of the front of the car when it is facing the left, stop pinching the right thumb against the right middle finger and pull the hands apart.

You should now have two loops on the right index. Push the top loop, the driver's head, to the tip of the index with the right thumb. Pull hard away with the left hand and nod the right index to let the top loop slip off. He should run away and the twang of the string should make a very good sound effect!

REPEAT WITH VARIATIONS

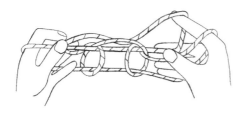

'Oh, no, someone has sat on the roof!'
Loosen hold on right index.

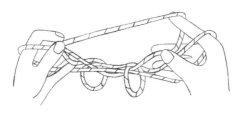

'Now someone very heavy has sat inside!'
Push pinched fingers closer.

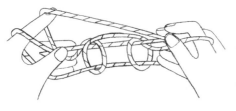

'Look! The car has changed direction!'
Lift the left index and drop the right.

...GO!

'Hey, wait for me!'

says the driver who

then runs after it.

Did you hear him go?

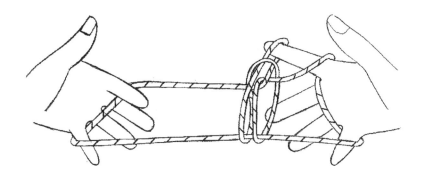

THE DRIVER

FIGURES INVENTED BY CHILDREN

STRING TRICKS

HINTS FOR PERFORMERS

AND TEACHERS

ORIGINS AND ACKNOWLEDGEMENTS

MAKING A FISH
by Jessica Wright, aged 9

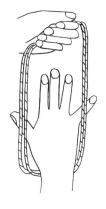

Left hand holds doubled loop. Right hand passes upright through the loop and returns — except for right thumb and little finger which, outstretched, catch sides of loop.
Left hand pulls away and then releases loop which swings onto right forearm.

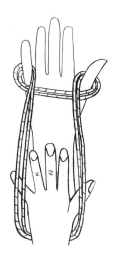

Left hand claps right forearm through loop and returns, except for outstretched thumb and little finger which catch sides of loop.

The fish tank is ready.

In the fish tank

a fish opens and

closes its mouth,

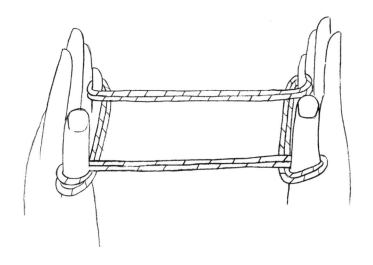

THE FISH TANK

A TALKING FISH

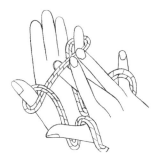

Right middle finger takes left palm strings from below.

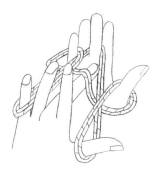

Left middle finger takes right palm strings from below.

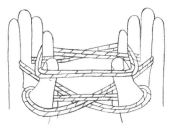

Thumbs go over middle finger loops to take near little finger strings from below.

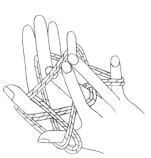

Right middle finger takes left palm string from below.

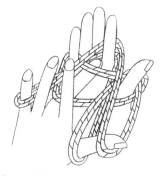

Left middle finger takes right palm string from below.

Little fingers tap to make fish mouth open and close (opposite page).

saying 'Fish!

Fish! Fish!'

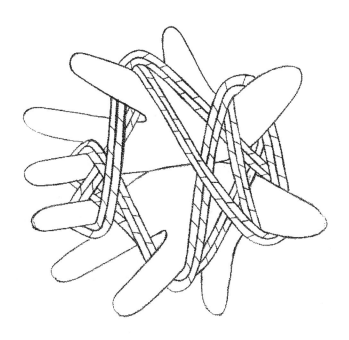

THE TALKING FISH

A MONKEY CHAIN VARIATION
by Raphael Taylor, aged 8.

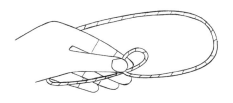

Make a small loop in the string. (A 'magnifying glass').

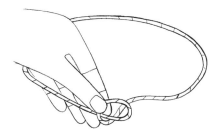

Place this small loop over the uppermost continuation of string close to the loop. ('Examine the string').

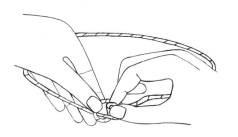

Pull this string a small way through the loop to make a new small loop. Hold onto this new small loop.

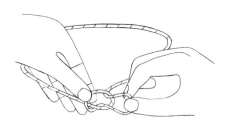

Two long strings extend from the figure. Pull one and the knot at its base is tightened. (Pull the other and the small loop is made still smaller.)

The string scoubidou is a variation of the monkey chain...

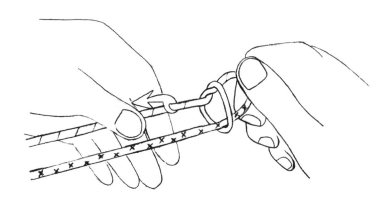

THE STRING SCOUBIDOU

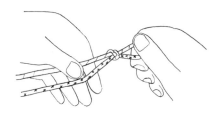

Pull the appropriate long string to tighten the knot.

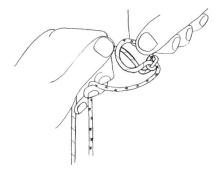

Then push this string through the small loop to make a new small loop. Hold onto this new loop and repeat.

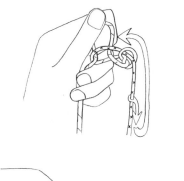

If you start at the junction of two colours the instructions are easy:
Push blue through red. Pull red.
Push red through blue. Pull blue.
Push blue ... etc.

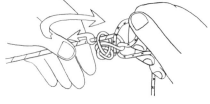

It can be used to make

all sorts of string models.

THE SCOUBIDOU

ROBOTS, BEARDS AND KNOTS

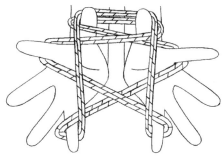

THE ROBOT
by Kavan Miller, aged 10.
Make Opening 'A' with a
doubled loop.
Thumbs go over index
loop to take far little
finger strings from below.

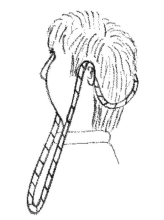

**FATHER CHRISTMAS'
BEARD**
by Gareth Hilton, aged 4.
Place your head in the
loop and tuck the side
strings over your ears.

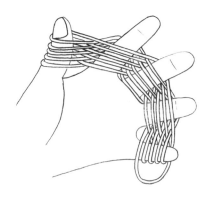

THE GLOVE
by Adam Blatchley, aged 6.
Wind a single strand in
and out of each finger.
Once the thumb or little
finger is reached continue
around and return,
winding the string the
other way.

THE NEVER-ENDING KNOT
by James Bartlett, aged 9.
Make Opening 'A' and swap loops.
Place right thumb loop on right little finger over the little finger loop.
Place right little finger loop on the right thumb.
Do the same on the left.
Swap index loops. Repeat the process several times.
Note that with each swap one loop goes through the other.

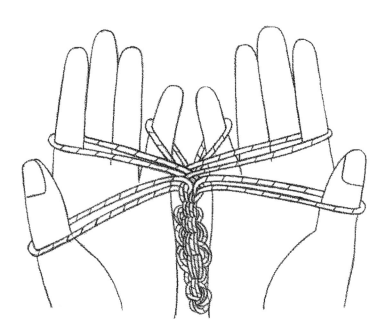

THE TRAMPOLINE AND OTHER FIGURES

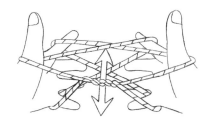

THE TRAMPOLINE
by Sandy Hagenbach, aged 8.
Place loop on thumbs. Rotate one thumb. Make Opening 'A'. Twist hands, moving thumbs apart and together to make trampoline bounce.

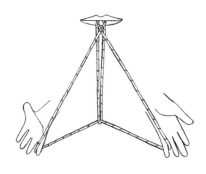

THE KITE
by Auren Lake Edwards, aged 8.
Make the Trampoline with a single complete twist.Mouth takes far thumb strings where they cross in the centre. Release thumbs and index to form Kite.

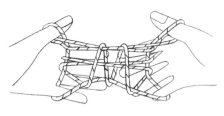

CAT'S EARS
by Florance Van Rinkhuyzen, aged 8.
Make the Trampoline with a single complete twist. Little fingers go over index and far thumb strings to pick up near thumb strings from below. Old little finger loops drop over new loops.

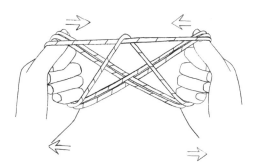

THE CAMERA by Danny Young, aged 10.
Make the Trampoline with a single twist.
Remove index and little finger loops, and put them, upturned on the thumbs. Widen thumb loops by entering all four fingers from the far side.
Twist hands to 'take photographs'.

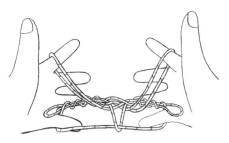

THE EAGLE by Raphael Taylor, aged 6.
1. Make the Trampoline with a single complete twist.
2. Thumbs go over index loop to pick up near little finger strings from below and return.
3. Middle fingers go over index loop to pick up far thumb strings from below and return.
4. Drop thumb strings, thumbs take middle finger loops from below, and remove middle fingers.
5. Repeat 2, 3 and 4 four times.
6. Release thumb loops to make the Eagle.

THE MAGIC FLAG

Just follow the drawings

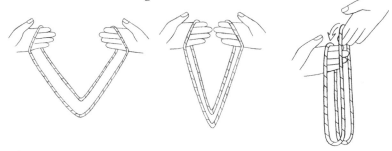

The MAGIC BOOK opens from above

and below.

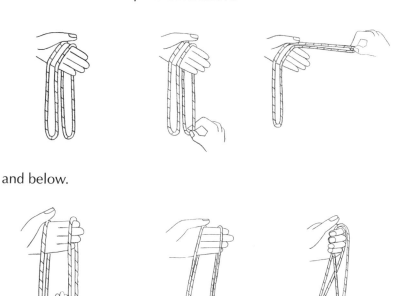

In it is a FLAG which changes colour!

This flag changes

colour as it flaps.

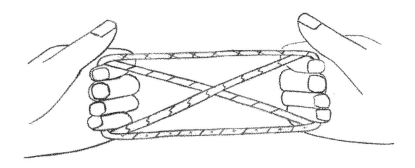

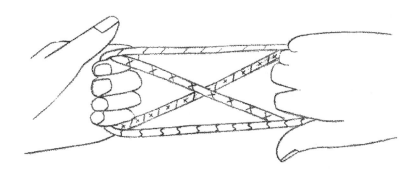

THE MAGIC FLAG

A PALM TRICK

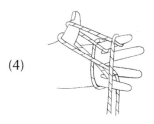

(1)

Hang loop on left palm (1).

(2)

(4)

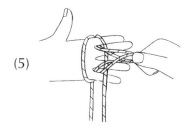

Bring the hanging string that went between the index and middle fingers back around the index and over the palm (4).

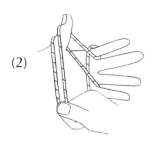

(3)

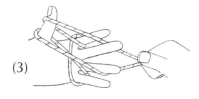

(5)

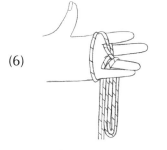

Bring the hanging string that is next to the index up between the index and middle fingers, and bring the hanging string that is near the little finger up between the little and ring fingers. Bring them between the index and thumb, around the thumb and back to where they came from (2 and 3).

(6)

Drop right hand strings. Remove thumb loops and place them between the middle and ring fingers (5 and 6). Pull palm string and the tangle disappears (opposite page).

First make a big tangle…

then watch it

disappear!

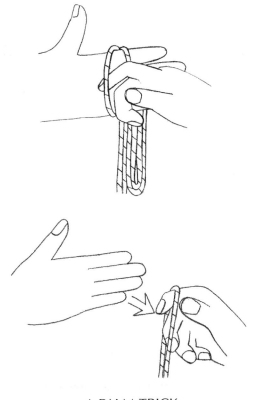

A PALM TRICK

THE NECKLACE

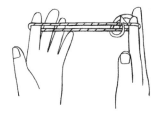

Place loop on index finger.

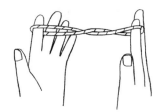

Rotate right index in one complete turn.

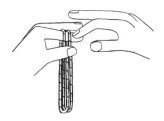

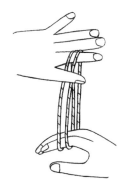

Place right index loop on left index.
Place right hand, palm down, into
the two hanging loops.
Move downwards and close fist.

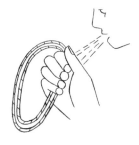

Release left hand. Blow on right hand and slowly open to reveal necklace link.

Separate the two strings to make the JUMPING FISH (see page 18).

Can you walk on stilts?

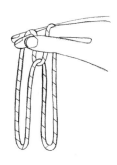

Ready to make a JUMPING FISH.

Feet in long loops make great STILTS!

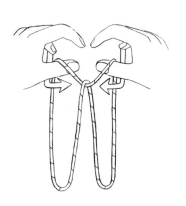

Make Opening 'A' from here...

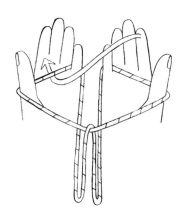

... to get to the Trampoline.

THE VOLCANO...

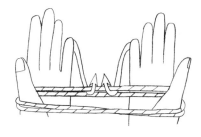

Double the string (see page 46).

Place loops on thumbs. Little fingers enter one of the far thumb strings from below.

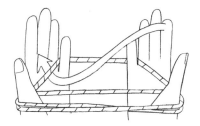

Right index takes left palm string from below. Repeat with left index to make a modified Opening 'A'.

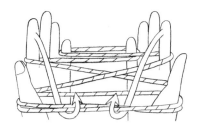

Right index enters thumb loops from above and lifts off near thumb strings.

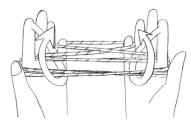

Index fingers rotate in three complete turns, first away towards little fingers, then up towards thumbs.

Hands come together slightly. Release little fingers. Middle, ring and little fingers enter index loops alongside index fingers and from beneath. Close fists.

This volcano is about

to ERUPT...

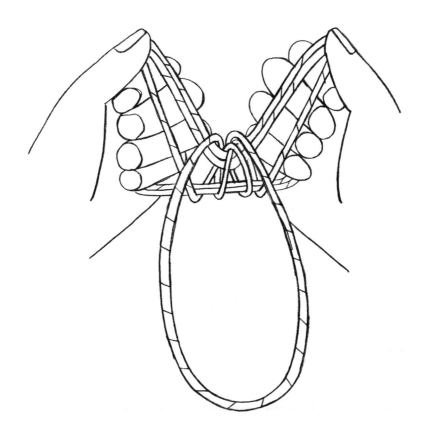

ERUPTS!

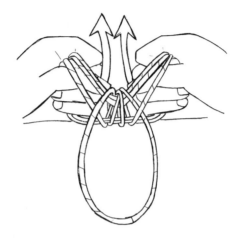

Ask a friend to hold out a thumb.
Lift the upper strings from the lower with the thumbs to make
the hanging loop unwind and jump onto your friend's thumb.

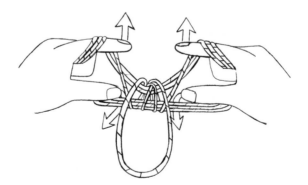

For extra power you can lift the upper strings with the index
while pushing the lower strings down with the thumbs.
If your string is too long start by trebling instead of doubling the
loop. If it is too short use an unmodified Opening 'A'.

Got you!

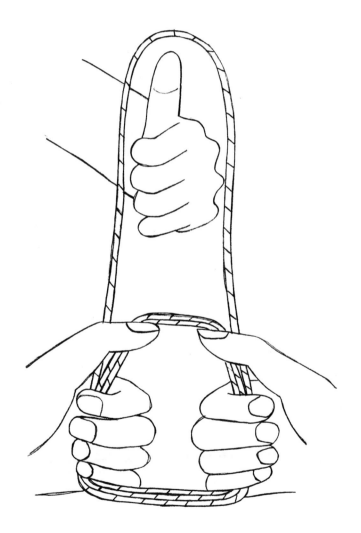

MAKING THE FROG

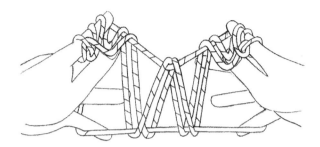

To make the Frog go directly from the Pig House to Eggs, missing out the Water Trough. You will only get four eggs but you will end up with a frog!

Alternatively you can make the Water Trough and then take the entry and exit strings of the 'W' instead of the sides. Then continue with all the instructions for the Pig.

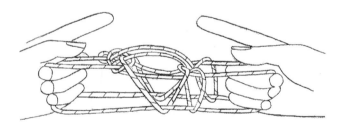

THE FROG

To make the shape better the thumb and index nearest to the frog's legs spread out the little finger strings from both sides.

To make an even more beautiful frog make the Gate with a trebled instead of a doubled loop. The two boys must climb the parallel strings and lift the far strings in three steps.
Continue with all the instructions for the Pig.

FROG AND TURTLE

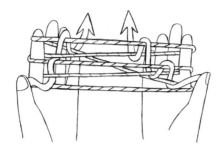

CLIMBING THE TREBLED GATE

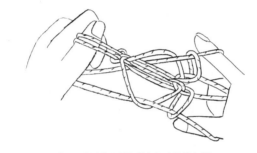

FROG SEEN FROM ABOVE

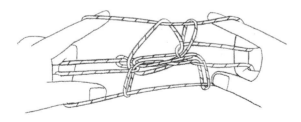

THE TURTLE

To make the Turtle, which is actually half a Pig and half a Frog, one thumb must take the entry strings of the 'W' while the other thumb takes the sides.

Then continue with all the instructions for the Pig. See drawing for method of final extension.

HINTS FOR PERFORMERS

A good way to start your performance is with a trick like the Volcano or with something attention-grabbing like throwing and popping bubbles (see next page)!

Then you can tell some stories. If you show the Little Bat make sure that you pause before it opens its wings and flies away. Then you can repeat the process.

If you show the Water Trough you can hold up the figure and ask what letter it looks like. When someone answers 'W' you can turn it upside down and tell them that it is really an 'M'.

The Racing Car can be repeated several times with variations. An extra long string can be used to make the Man Climbing the Tree more effective. If you repeat the verse several times your audience might learn it before the man reaches the top! Then you can get some more audience participation with Sawing Together.

Once the tree has fallen and your partner has been applauded everyone will be eager to be given strings and learn some tricks.

Here's a Bubble ...Pop It!

To make a bubble:

Turn, lift and let go!

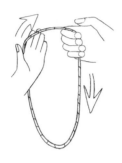 

THROWING A SPINNING BUBBLE

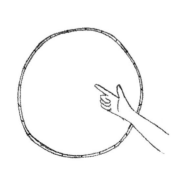 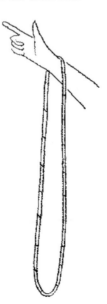

POPPING IT!

HINTS FOR TEACHERS

Once you have given out strings using the Magic Handshake or by Throwing the Frisbee (simply the Bubble made with a doubled loop) you can teach some tricks.

A group of four- or five-year-olds can learn the Jumping Fish, the Magic Book and the Magic Flag and they can walk around on Stilts. They may enjoy making the Glove while singing 'In and out of the dusty bluebells' and some can make the Monkey Chain.

A group of six-, seven- and eight-year-olds can learn Sawing Together, the Bow and Arrow and the Man Climbing the Tree. Each of these figures starts with the same opening. Cutting the Hand is also a great one for beginners (see Book One), but make sure that the same hand moves first both times you make Opening 'A'.

Be prepared to move your students' fingers for them if necessary (hands learn more quickly than heads) and take every opportunity to teach just one person at a time. Then encourage that person to teach as well.

If a clever teenager learns your entire repertoire in a few minutes ask him or her to make the figures with eyes closed! Then get him or her to teach, to invent and to make up some credible stories. Or some incredible ones!

SAWING TOGETHER

Two people who know
Opening 'A' can
saw together.

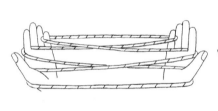

Make Opening 'A'.

2nd player takes the framing
strings...

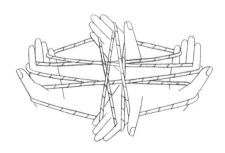

...and also makes Opening 'A'.

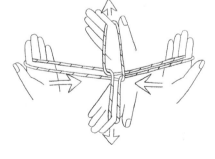

Both players keep index loops
only.

ORIGINS AND ACKNOWLEDGEMENTS

TRADITIONAL FIGURES

The Bow and Arrow is common in many parts of the world. In the Torres Straits it is called the Fish Spear. It is known as the Sea-Egg Spear on Vancouver Island and Pitching a Tent in British Columbia.

The Man Climbing a Tree is from the original inhabitants of Queensland, Australia.

The Pig comes from New Caledonia.

Both the Little Bat and the Frog come from Guiana, South America.

The Bird's Nest is a figure from the Navaho people of North America.

Sawing Together is common throughout the world. Two other methods of making this figure are given in Book One.

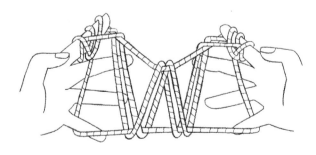

LITTLE FISHES
From the Torres Straits, between Papua New Guinea and Australia.

126

THE WATER TROUGH...

The Water Trough

is found all around

the Pacific.

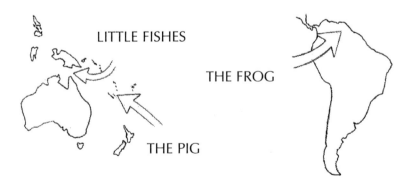

In the Torres Straits it is called LITTLE FISHES. On the island of Lifu, Loyalty Islands, New Caledonia it becomes the PIG. In Guiana, South America, it turns into the FROG.

ORIGINS AND ACKNOWLEDGEMENTS

OTHER FIGURES

The Palm Trick was first shown to me by my father, Brian Taylor. It is common throughout the world and has some variations.

The Flag was first shown to me by Davot Irving when he was 14. The Necklace was shown to me by my niece, Holly Taylor when she was 5. When you try and make the Frog you sometimes end up with the Turtle, as discovered and shown to me by Eve Jones when she was 9. My son, Raphael, aged 8, discovered how special the Frog could be when made with a modified opening. Freddie Gullivar showed me how to get from the Treasure Box to the Necklace when he was 9. Other children's inventions are acknowledged separately.

The flying action of the Bat, the turning of the Bird's Nest into the Racing Car and the Volcano are my own discoveries.

A LAST SEQUENCE:
Using the instructions from this book try the following sequence: Book, Flag, Girl, Necklace, Jumping Fish, Trampoline, Camera.

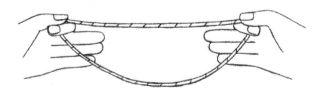

SMILE PLEASE!

A last figure:

Find the girl's necklace!

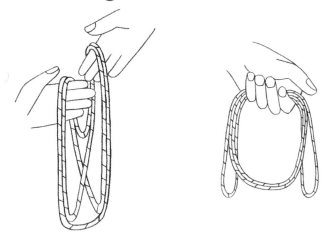

Make the Magic Flag and call it the Treasure Box. Fold it as if it was the Book. Now you have the Girl.

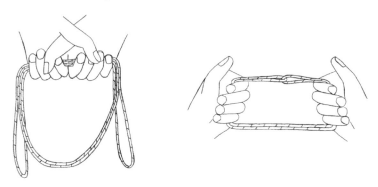

Hold Girl's Head in both hands.
Separate the hands to find her Necklace.

MAKE YOUR OWN LOOP
(With adult supervision)

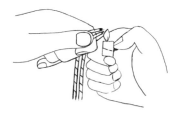

Melt together the slightly frayed ends of a 2 metre length of nylon cord. *Don't get burnt!*

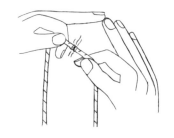

Push ends together. After 5 seconds they hold.

Squeeze and turn rapidly while still hot.

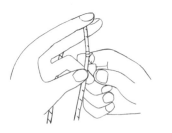

Repeat to smooth join.

Buy nylon cord from a hardware shop and use clothes dye for rainbow colours.

FORTHCOMING BOOK

String Games and Stories Book Three
by Michael Taylor

'Who are you?' says the Talking Mouth

Mind the Coconut doesn't fall on your head... Too late!

Watch a Sunflower growing... When you water it!

Take a Caribou for a walk...

Make a figure with two strings

Make a sun and star with several friends

More children's inventions and tricks

And make this Scoubidou
Man with a single string
loop!

BIBLIOGRAPHY

String Figures and how to make them
by Caroline Furness Jayne.
ISBN 0 486 20152 X
Dover Books, first published in 1905!

Cat's Cradle, Owl's Eyes: A Book of String Games
by Camilla Gryski.
ISBN 0 688 03941 3
Beech Tree Books.

String Games from around the World
by Anne Akers Johnson.
ISBN 1 57054 040 3.
Klutz.

Fascinating String Figures
by the International String Figure Association.
ISBN 0 486 40400 5
Dover Books.

The International String Figure Association
The ISFA publishes a wonderful quarterly magazine, twice-yearly newsletter and annual journal. For more information write to:
ISFA Press, P.O. Box 5134,
Pasadena, California 91117, USA
E-mail: webweavers@isfa.org
World-Wide-Web: www.isfa.org

ABOUT THE AUTHOR

Michael Taylor is a teacher and movement specialist who promotes traditional childhood skills-games of movement and agility for the classroom, playground and gym which aid co-ordination and are developmental and fun.

His string figure stories have been presented in hospitals, schools, old people's homes and summer camps. One story, 'The Dragon, the Princess and Jack' was specially translated by Claudine, his wife, and shown at the 1st Traditional Games Festival in Berck-sur-mer.

As well as string figures he collects and teaches clapping games, finger games, jump-rope activities, ball bouncing and bean bag games. Some of these will be published in future books.

Michael Taylor has worked in schools with teachers and in hospitals with nurses and play therapists. He gives occasional parties for children – sometimes with his son, Raphael, as his special helper!

More information on INSET (workshops and training) and bulk orders of strings can be obtained from:

Michael Taylor,
9 Kidbrooke Rise
Forest Row
East Sussex
RH18 5LA, UK.

OTHER BOOKS FROM HAWTHORN PRESS

Pull the Other One!
String Games and Stories Book 1
Michael Taylor

This well-travelled and entertaining series of tales is
accompanied by clear instructions and explanatory
diagrams – guaranteed not to tie you in knots and will
teach you tricks with which to dazzle your friends! With
something for everyone, these ingenious tricks and tales
are developed and taught with utter simplicity, making
them suitable from age 5 upwards.
128pp; 216 x 148mm;1 869 890 49 3; paperback.

All Year Round
Ann Druitt, Christine Fynes-Clinton, Marije Rowling

Brimming with things to make; activities, stories, poems and songs to share with your
family. Observing the round of festivals is an enjoyable way to bring rhythm into
children's lives and provide a series of meaningful landmarks to look forward to.
320pp; 250 x 200mm; 1 869 890 47 7; paperback.

The Children's Year
Crafts and Clothes for Children and Parents to make
Stephanie Cooper, Christine Fynes-Clinton, Marije Rowling

Children and parents are encouraged to try all sorts of handwork, with different
projects relating to the seasons of the year.
192pp; 250 x 200mm; 1 869 890 00 0; paperback.

Festivals, Family and Food
Diana Carey and Judy Large

A unique source of stories, recipes, things to make,
activities, poems, songs and festivals.
224pp; 250 x 200mm; 0 950 706 23 X; paperback.

Festivals Together
A Guide to Multicultural Celebration
Sue Fitzjohn, Minda Weston, Judy Large

This special book for families and teachers helps you
celebrate festivals from cultures from all over the world.
224pp; 250 x 200mm; 1 869 890 46 9; paperback.